"Entering Into His Promises"

An Inductive Study
in
The Book of Joshua

"Pass through the camp and command the people,
saying, 'Prepare provisions for yourselves,
for within three days you will cross over this Jordan,
to go in to possess the land which the LORD your God
is giving you to possess.'" Joshua 1:11

Published By
Morningstar Christian Chapel
Whittier, California 90603

"Entering Into His Promises"
An Inductive Study in The Book of Joshua
Copyright © 2005 by Morningstar Christian Chapel
Published by Morningstar Christian Chapel
ISBN: 978-0-9729477-3-2

Additional copies of this book are available by contacting:

Morningstar Christian Chapel
Whittier, California 90603
562.943.0297

Introduction to Joshua

> "Pass through the camp and command the people, saying, 'Prepare provisions for yourselves, for within three days you will cross over this Jordan, to go in to possess the land which the LORD your God is giving you to possess.'" Joshua 1:11

The book of Joshua is the book of new beginnings. It is the first of the twelve historical books of the Old Testament.

After forty years of wandering in the wilderness, the Lord brought His people into the Promised Land, to their inheritance, which He had prepared for them.

Similarly, we too, are in need of a new beginning and God would have His children to enter in and experience the peace and rest of the Promised Land, even as we battle the enemies that still remain.

Through the conquest of the Land of Canaan, the children of Israel learned that victory comes to those who go forward with their faith and hope in God, and walk in obedience to His Word.

The events recorded in the Book of Joshua have to do with the life of God's people, not their death. The Promised Land is sometimes mistakenly compared to Heaven. The Promised Land was to those in Joshua's day a place of deliverance from the bondage of Egypt, a land given to them by God. But, the battles would continue – just as they do today in the life of the Christian who has been brought out of the bondage of the world.

The book is named after the one who God called to lead this chosen people. His name was originally Hoshea, which means Salvation. In Numbers 13:16 we are told that Moses changed it to Yehoshua, which means Yahweh is Salvation. He is also called, Yeshua, the Hebrew equivalent of the Greek name translated Jesus. Joshua is a type of Jesus. In his role of leading the people into their possessions, he foreshadows the One who will bring many sons to glory.. (Hebrews 2:10).

Joshua was born as a slave in Egypt and became a mighty conqueror in Canaan. He led the Israelites in the defeat of the Amalekites just two months after they had come out of Egypt. He

INTRODUCTION CONTINUED...

ENTERING
into **His** **Promises**

served as the personal attendant to Moses, as one of the twelve spies, and then was called by the Lord to take Moses' position as the leader of the children of Israel.

The entire book of Joshua describes the entering, conquest and possession of the land of Canaan. As Joshua led the people into the Promised Land, we too can share in the inheritance because we are blessed with all spiritual blessings in the heavenly places in Christ (Ephesians 1:3). Sadly, many believers chose to live like paupers rather than the King's kids.

We can divide the Book into two parts; chapters 1-12 cover the conquest of the land and chapters 13-24 detail the settlement of the land. The key verses are considered to be Joshua 1:8 and 11:23.

As we begin this study, are you looking to be set free from the bondage of the world? Do you need to enter into His rest? Have you claimed your inheritance through faith in Jesus Christ? It's time to possess your possessions! It's time to cross over...to go in...to possess that which the Lord your God has given you to possess (Joshua 1:8).

Outline of Joshua

Joshua

I. The Conquest of the Land.................Chapters 1-12

   A. The Lord Prepares the Nation (1-5)

     1. Joshua is appointed (1)
     2. The spies sent into the Land (2)
     3. The river opens (3)
     4. A memorial at Gilgal (4)
     5. Spiritually preparing for battle (5)

   B. The Battle Belongs to the Lord (6-12)

     1. God's victory at Jericho (6)
     2. The people's defeat at Ai (7)
     3. Ai conquered God's way (8)
     4. Deceived by the Gibeonites (9)
     5. Victory in the South (10)
     6. Conquest of the North (11)
     7. All the Conquered Kings (12)

II. The Settlement of the Land..............Chapters 13-24

   A. Claiming God's Promises (13-22)

     1. East of the Jordon (13)
     2. West of the Jordon (14-19)
     3. Cities of refuge established (20)
     4. Hometown for the Levites (21)
     5. Rueben, Gad, half of Manasseh return home (22)

   B. God's call of Commitment (23-24)

     1. Final words to the leaders (23)
     2. Final words to the God's people (24)

ENTERING *into* *His* **PROMISES**

Lesson Index

DAY 1 ~ BEGIN IN PRAYER

1. Read Joshua Chapters 1-12.

2. What is your impression of this first half of Joshua based on this reading?

3. Do you see any reoccurring themes or phrases that help you to evaluate the author's reasons for writing?

4. What lesson can you apply to your Christian walk today?

DAY 2 ~ BEGIN IN PRAYER

1. Read Joshua 13-24.

2. What is your impression of this second half of Joshua based on this reading?

3. Do you see any reoccurring themes or phrases that help you to evaluate the author's reasons for writing?

4. In the book of Joshua much is said about overcoming the enemy. How does this apply to your life today?

DAY 3 ~ BEGIN IN PRAYER

1. Read Chapters 1-6. Give a 4-6 word title to each chapter to help you remember its contents.

Chapter 1

Chapter 2

CONTINUED...

into **ENTErING**
His **promises**

Chapter 3

Chapter 4

Chapter 5

Chapter 6

DAY 4 – BEGIN IN PRAYER

1.   Read Chapters 7-12. Give a title to each chapter.

Chapter 7

Chapter 8

Chapter 9

Chapter 10

Chapter 11

Chapter 12

DAY 5 – BEGIN IN PRAYER

1.   Read Chapters 13-18. Give a title to each chapter.

Chapter 13

Chapter 14

Chapter 15

Chapter 16

Chapter 17

Chapter 18

DAY 6 – BEGIN IN PRAYER

1.   Read Chapters 19-24. Give a title to each chapter.

Chapter 19

Chapter 20

Chapter 21

Chapter 22

Chapter 23

Chapter 24

4

Notes

_____

_____

_____

_____

_____

_____

_____

_____

_____

_____

_____

_____

_____

_____

_____

_____

_____

_____

_____

_____

_____

_____

_____

DAY 1 – BEGIN IN PRAYER

1.   Read Joshua 1.

     What promises do you find that encourage you today?

     What exhortations are given that you can apply to your Christian walk?

2.   Read Joshua 2.

     What impresses you about the account of Rahab and the spies?

     What questions arise that you may want to discuss later?

3.   Use Joshua 1:7 as your memory verse for this week. Write it out and begin memorizing it today.

DAY 2 – BEGIN IN PRAYER

1.   Read Joshua 1.

2.   Re-read Joshua 1:1-9.

3.   Let's do a bit of background study on the preparation of this man the LORD has chosen to succeed Moses and lead the children of Israel into the Promised Land. What do you learn from the following Scriptures about his life and how might these experiences have helped make him a great leader?

     a. Exodus 17:9-13

     b. Exodus 24:9-13

     c. Exodus 33:11

CONTINUED...

into His **ENTERING** **promises**

d. Numbers 13:16 & 14:6-10

e. Deuteronomy 34:9

Personal: Have you ever felt frustrated by the circumstances in your life? Can you see that they are being used by the Lord to shape you and make you ready for even greater service? It took 40 years of submission in training before Joshua got this call from God!

4. God speaks to Joshua saying, "Moses My servant is dead. Now therefore, arise, go over this Jordon, you and all this people, to the land which I am giving to them – the children of Israel." What promises are given to Joshua in verses 3-6?

What similar promise, encouragement, and exhortation is given to the believer in Jesus Christ today?

a. Matthew 28:19, 20

b. Romans 8:31-35

c. Hebrews 13:5, 6

d. Hebrews 4:1, 2 & 10, 11

5. What does verse 3 tell us about when this giving of the land happened?

God had already given the land to them, yet they still needed to go in and possess it by faith. It would take time, and it required forward progress...they would have to step out in faith and obedience, following the clear direction of the LORD. They were instructed to observe and do all the LORD had commanded. What do we learn regarding the importance of obedience in our walk with the Lord?

a. 1 John 3:23, 24

b. Revelation 22:14

Why do you think God repeats the exhortation, "Be strong and courageous," three times in four verses (vs. 6-9)?

6. How has studying the calling of Joshua encouraged you to step out and possess your possessions? Has the enemy overrun a portion of your land? Be strong and courageous and fight the good fight – beginning today!

7. Record Joshua 1:7 here and continue to commit it to memory. As you do, make it the prayer of your heart this week!

DAY 3 – BEGIN IN PRAYER

1. Read Joshua 1.

2. Re-read Joshua 1:10-18.

3. God had given this people the land but it was their responsibility to possess it. Joshua decisively commands the officers to instruct the people to prepare provisions for themselves. Joshua told the people to be ready to move, to pack their food, and to prepare their families. He had been present when God delivered the nation from Egypt and he had confidence that God would work on their behalf again. What direction did God give to the prior generation in Exodus 14:13, 14 when He brought them out of Egypt?

Crossing the Jordon River would mean the last of the pillar of fire and cloud,

CONTINUED...

and the last of the manna. It would represent the death of the flesh and a new walk by faith. What do you learn from the following Scriptures about your inheritance in Christ?

a. Matthew 5:3, 5

b. Matthew 19:29, 30

c. Romans 8:15-17

d. Philippians 3:20, 21

e. 1 Peter 1:3-5

4. Two lessons stand out in Joshua's directions: the people could not accomplish this task alone and they had a clear responsibility to participate in God's work. He told the leaders to go and prepare, and he gave a specific exhortation to the men of the two and a half tribes who were going to inhabit the land on the east of the Jordan. What were these men to do and how does it speak to us about our responsibility to care for the needs of the Body of Christ?

Optional Challenge Question (Dig Deeper): Why did these two and half tribes not cross the Jordon and enter in to the Promised Land? What risk is taken when we choose to dwell on the border?

5. The leaders answered Joshua with declaration of commitment to his leadership. What did they declare according to verses 16-18?

What is our responsibility, as Christians, to those whom the Lord has set up in places of authority and as leaders in the church?

    a. 1 Timothy 2:1-3

    b. Hebrews 13:7, 17, 18

    c. 1 Peter 2:13-15

6. How has today's lesson encouraged you to walk by faith? What possessions are yours that you haven't yet appropriated? Are you trying to live across the border and wondering why you have no rest? How are you being a support to those leaders God has placed in your life?

7. Record Joshua 1:7 here and continue to commit it to memory.

DAY 4 – BEGIN IN PRAYER

1. Read Joshua 2.

2. Re-read Joshua 2:1-7.

3. Joshua makes a decision to send spies into Jericho. This plan had not worked too well for Moses when 10 of the 12 spies convinced the people the challenge was impossible. Their judgment caused the entire generation (except Caleb and Joshua) to die in the wilderness. Joshua decides to send two and their report is far more faithful. What was their conclusion according to Joshua 2:24?

    What encouragement are you given when you face a seemingly impossible situation in your life?

    a. Genesis 18:13, 14

CONTINUED...

b. Job 42:2

c. Jeremiah 32:17

d. Luke 1:37

e. Luke 18:27

4. We read that Rahab had some convictions about the God of Israel and she chose to hide the spies from the king's messengers. What questionable method did she use to protect the spies? (vs.3-5)

Is there ever a time or a situation when lying is the right thing to do?

Based on the truths you have learned today, could God have spared these spies without Rabab's action?

5. How do the following Scriptures answer the question regarding lying and how do they help you to evaluate the decisions you make in your speech?

a. Proverbs 12:22

b. John 8:44

c. Colossians 3:9

    d. Ephesians 4:25

6. How has your faith in the Lord's ability to handle the battles you face been strengthened today? Will you remember to speak the truth in love? Don't fall prey to the tools of the enemy who is the "father of lies!"

7. Record Joshua 1:7 here and continue to commit it to memory.

DAY 5 – BEGIN IN PRAYER

1. Read Joshua 2.

2. Re-read Joshua 2:8-24.

3. We can see that even though Rahab made the wrong choice by lying, she did so based on her very limited knowledge and a budding faith in the LORD. What does she declare about Him in verses 9-11?

   What more do we learn about Rahab and how do these Scriptures clearly demonstrate God's grace and mercy?

   a. Matthew 1:5 & 16

   b. Hebrews 11:1, 2 & 31

   c. James 2:25, 26

4. God, in His amazing grace, uses people that we may never think would be

CONTINUED...

useful as His servants. This truth is beautifully illustrated in Rahab's life. Perhaps you've seen this in your life – would you have ever imagined that YOU could become the son or daughter of the King of Kings. How do the following Scriptures remind you of the Lord's ever-present grace, and His willingness to use you as you surrender to Him?

a. 1Corinthians 1:27-31

b. 2Corinthians 4:6, 7

c. 1Peter 2:9-12

5. Rahab's action in protecting the spies was motivated by her desire to protect herself and her family. She had heard of the power of the God of Israel. The word had spread about how He had dried up the Red Sea (40 years earlier), and how the people of God had destroyed great kingdoms. She feared and believed, and begged for mercy. She received it! What was she to do to protect her family?

How was this act similar to the Passover in Egypt (Exodus 12:7-13)?

The scarlet cord is symbolic of the blood. In Exodus the blood on the doorposts protected the inhabitants from certain death. In our lives the blood shed by Jesus Christ on the cross at Calvary spares the believer from eternal death. What do you learn about the shedding of blood that causes you to rejoice today?

a. Ephesians 2:13

b. Hebrews 10:19

c. Revelation 1:5

6. Think back to where the Lord has brought you from – how has He blessed your life through the shedding of His blood? How is He leading you to step out in His grace and mercy?

7. Record Joshua 1:7 – you should be able to do it from memory!

DAY 6 ~ BEGIN IN PRAYER

1. Read Joshua Chapters 1 and 2.

2. Write a prayer asking the Lord to use the truths in these two chapters to change and motivate your walk of faith with Him.

3. Record Joshua 1:7 without looking!

Ps 119:97 - Oh, how I love Your law! It is my meditation all the day.

Notes

_____

_____

_____

_____

_____

_____

_____

_____

_____

_____

_____

_____

_____

_____

_____

_____

_____

_____

_____

_____

_____

_____

_____

DAY 1 – BEGIN IN PRAYER

1. Read Joshua 3.

   What are the main details of the event that is recorded in chapter 3?

   What lesson is there to be learned that you can apply to your walk of faith today?

2. Read Joshua 4.

   What are the main details of the event that is recorded in chapter 4?

   What does the memorial of stones represent and how is the importance of this action still vital for us, as Christians, today?

3. Use Joshua 3:3 as your memory verse for this week. Write it out and begin memorizing it today.

DAY 2 – BEGIN IN PRAYER

1. Read Joshua 3.

2. Re-read Joshua 3:1-6.

3. The LORD had spoken to Joshua assuring him that He had called him to step up and lead His people into the Promised Land. The spies had gone in and come out with a faithful report of how the people feared the hand of the Lord and their report encouraged Joshua's faith. Joshua rose early and moved this people, who numbered in the millions, up to the banks of the Jordon. This journey was approximately 10 miles. For three days the people camped and

CONTINUED...

into His **ENTERING Promises**

viewed an obstacle that stopped the forward progress of their journey. What might the people have been thinking during these three days and how might it compare to the seemingly impassable obstacles in your life today?

What example is given for us to follow in the lives of the following men of faith regarding our inability and God's ability?

a. 2Chronicles 20:12

b. Romans 4:17-21

c. 2Corinthians 1:8-10

After three days the officers commanded the people to turn their full attention toward something other than the raging river that they could not cross on their own. Who and what were the people to follow? (v.3)

4.   What do you learn about the Ark of the Covenant from the following references?

a. Exodus 25:10-22

b. Hebrews 9:4

The people were to follow the Ark of the Covenant. It represented the LORD's presence among the people. They were to maintain a distance of about 1000 yards behind this very holy object. They were to follow, but not so closely that others would lose sight of the way. What was different about the place where they would now be heading? (v.4)

5.   What was Joshua's message to the people in verse 5?

In his words there was both a command and a promise; and the fulfillment of the promise would depend on their obedience to the command. They were to sanctify themselves. To sanctify means to be set apart, to be consecrated, to be dedicated for a purpose or person. Israel did this before God at Mt. Sinai and now they were to do it again in preparation for seeing the LORD do mighty wonders among them. This picture of necessary sanctification in the life of the believer is carried into the New Testament as well. What do we learn about our obligation to sanctify ourselves?

a. 2Corinthians 6:14 – 7:1

b. Ephesians 4:26, 27

c. Colossians 3:8-14

6.   Are there any seemingly impossible obstacles in your life? Are your eyes on the situation or on the Deliverer Who is leading and guiding your life? He may be leading you into places you have never been but as you seek His will and surrender to His Spirit, He is going before you each step of the way. Will you sanctify your heart and life in order to see the mighty works He wants to accomplish through you?

CONTINUED...

7. Record Joshua 3:3 here and continue to work on committing it to memory!

DAY 3 — BEGIN IN PRAYER

1. Read Joshua 3.

2. Re-read Joshua 3:7-17.

3. In verse 7 the LORD said to Joshua, "This day I will begin to exalt you in the sight of all Israel, that they may know that, as I was with Moses, so I will be with you." These words to Joshua were a foreshadowing (a type) of the Holy One to come, Who would be reavealed by His Father very near this same place. Record what you learn from the following references.

    a. Matthew 3:13-17

    b. John 1:26-34

4. The LORD reveals His plan to Joshua. It wouldn't have been a surprise to Joshua because he'd seen God do a similar work when he was a much younger man. What command was Joshua to give to the priests? (v. 8)

    How have these others taken bold steps of faith in obedience to the direction of the LORD?

    a. Genesis 6:13 & 22

    b. Genesis 12:1-4

    c. 1Samuel 14:1-7

    d. Acts 14:1-7

Personal: What is He calling you to do "in faith"?

5.   It is a characteristic of a strong, spiritual leader that his every word and action gives all the glory to God alone. According to verse 10, what was one of the purposes for this miracle of the parting of the Jordon River?

God honors faith, but He doesn't expect us to follow blindly. Joshua and the priests acted in faith based on the sure, spoken Word of God. He told them to go and they trusted Him and obeyed. We have that very same sure foundation in His written Word today. Therefore, our every thought, word and step must be based upon His truth, or we might be led astray by our feelings or our experiences. What do you learn about His Word, and how will it help you in your walk today?

a. Romans 15:4

b. Hebrews 4:12

c. 2Timothy 3:16, 17

d. 2Peter 1:19-21

6.   Can you recall a time in your life that you saw the Lord "part the Jordon" reminding you of His mighty and awesome sovereignty over circumstances? How important is God's Word to you? Do you depend upon it to lead, guide and strengthen you everyday? The Lord desires to use you to accomplish His purposes but we must remember that when He does – it is for His glory and His glory only!

7.   Record Joshua 3:3 here and continue to work on committing it to memory!

DAY 4 ~ BEGIN IN PRAYER

1. Read Joshua 4.

2. Re-read Joshua 4:1-9.

3. Two piles of stone were set up as memorials of Israel's crossing of the Jordon: one at Gilgal and one in the midst of the Jordon where the priests had stood with the Ark of the Covenant. What was the purpose of these memorials?

    Why do you think they would need to be reminded?

    What are a few other memorials that we have seen established in the Old Testament?

    a. Exodus 12:12-14

    b. Exodus 28:9-12

    c. Numbers 10:10

4. Who was the LORD most interested in getting the message to regarding His mighty works on behalf of His people?

    Why do you think this translation of faith and reverence was (and is) so important?

    What exhortation is found in the following Scriptures and how can you apply it to your daily walk with the Lord?

    a. Deuteronomy 4:9

b. Deuteronomy 6:4-9

c. Psalm 78:1-7

d. Ephesians 6:4

Personal: Is your faith alive and active and are you doing all that you can to show the children in your life (sons, daughters, nieces, nephews, grandchildren, students, and neighbors) the mighty works of the Lord so that they will want to follow Him, too?

5.   What "memorials" have we been given in the church today that remind us of God's work on our behalf in bringing us out of the bondage of sin and giving us access to intimate fellowship with Him through the sacrifice of His Son?

a. Romans 6:4

b. 1Corinthians 11:23-26

6.   Think back to what the Lord has accomplished in your life, from where has He brought you? What has He done for you? How have you taken it for granted or slipped away from being so diligent? What more can you do to display God's love and power to others in your life? (If you have not yet asked Jesus to be the Lord and Savior of your life, you can do so now – See Romans 6:23, 10:13 and 10:9,10)

7.   Record Joshua 3:3 here and continue to work on committing it to memory!

DAY 5 – BEGIN IN PRAYER

1.   Read Joshua 4.

CONTINUED...

2. Re-read Joshua 4:10-24.

3. The people had all crossed over, the twelve stones were collected from the Jordon, Joshua built a second memorial in the midst of the river, and the priests stepped out of the riverbed. Only then did the waters of the Jordon return to their place and overflow their banks. How could this not change the people's hearts and lives forever! It was the tenth day of the first month (four days before Passover). Where did they make camp?

    In later years, Gilgal became an important center for the nation. What were some of the events that occurred at Gilgal?

    a. 1Samuel 11:15

    b. 1Samuel 7:15, 16

    c. 2Kings 4:38-44

4. Sadly, this memorial would gradually lose its spiritual meaning. Instead of remembering God's might and power the people would begin to worship idols in Gilgal. Such worship was forbidden. Read Judges 2:8-15, what heartbreaking details are given about the failure of this people to teach their children to follow the LORD?

    Joshua had reminded the people all that Moses had commanded them! What warning were they given?

    a. Deuteronomy 6:12-15

    b. Deuteronomy 8:7-14

5. Likewise, what warning are we given, as followers of the Lord Jesus Christ,

that when heeded will keep us from falling?

   a. Colossians 2:8-10

   b. Hebrews 10:35-39

   c. 2Peter 3:14-18

   d. 1John 2:15-17

6.   We have been given God's Word to lead, guide, and protect us, and His Holy Spirit to teach, exhort and stir our hearts. Is there an area in your life that needs to be resubmitted to His Word and the Holy Spirit? Beware, because the enemy is seeking someone to devour! Do not allow him to gain a foothold in your life!

7.   Record Joshua 3:3 here and continue to work on committing it to memory!

DAY 6 – BEGIN IN PRAYER

1.   Read Joshua Chapters 3 and 4. (You can do it! – It's important!)

2.   Write a prayer asking the Lord to use the truths in these two chapters to change and motivate your walk of faith with Him.

3.   Record Joshua 3:3 without looking!

CONTINUED...

Notes

_____

_____

_____

_____

_____

_____

_____

_____

_____

_____

_____

_____

_____

_____

_____

_____

_____

_____

_____

_____

_____

_____

_____

DAY 1 – BEGIN IN PRAYER

1. Read Joshua 5.

    What are the main details recorded in chapter 5?

    Is there a warning to be heeded in chapter 5?

2. Read Joshua 6.

    What are the main details recorded in chapter 6?

    Is there a lesson to be applied from chapter 6?

3. Use Joshua 6:16 as your memory verse for this week. Write it out and begin memorizing it today.

DAY 2 – BEGIN IN PRAYER

1. Read Joshua 5.

2. Re-read Joshua 5:1-9.

3. What was the response of the kings of the Amorites and the kings of the Canaanites upon seeing the miracle of the parting of the Jordon River?

    How might their response have been an encouragement to the people who stood facing the enemy?

CONTINUED..

ENTERING *into His* **Promises**

What had they been told was a certainty according to Joshua 3:9-10?

4. The children of Israel camped at Gilgal facing a people whose hearts had been melted with fear. It seemed as though they should march in and conquer the city. However, there were spiritual preparations that needed to be addressed. What covenant had to be reestablished?

Who needed to be circumcised?

God had established the rite of circumcision with Abraham when he had called him out of paganism and made a covenant with him to give him a land, a people, and an eternal blessing. This sign of the covenant was to be a continuous practice for the people of Israel. What do we learn about circumcision from Genesis 17:9-14?

The covenant of circumcision was to symbolize the cutting away of the flesh and a total and complete consecration to the LORD. Through this ritual the Jews became a "marked people" because they belonged to the true and living God. Sadly, it would repeatedly become an action without any heart surrender. What strong words of exhortation are recorded in the following Scriptures?

a. Deuteronomy 10:12-16

b. Deuteronomy 30:6

c. Jeremiah 4:4

Food for thought: How would an operation that incapacitated all the fighting men for several days challenge the people's faith as they camped two miles from Jericho? How does this truth apply to your walk of faith today?

5. Remember, the Land of Promise represents our walk in the spirit. The covenant of circumcision for us, as Christians, represents our crucifying of the flesh and total surrender to the Lord Jesus Christ. What does the Lord teach us about the circumcision of the heart?

    a. Romans 2:28, 29

    b. Philippians 3:3

    c. Colossians 2:11-14

6. Are you standing on the promises of victory that you have been given in Christ? Do you need to study them more closely to increase your faith? God said He had given them the land (past tense), but they would have to enter in obedience and claim the promise – so do you and I! Have you been trusting in the flesh? Do you need to circumcise it – cut it off?

7. Record Joshua 6:16 here and continue to work on committing it to memory!

DAY 3 - BEGIN IN PRAYER

1. Read Joshua 5.

2. Re-read Joshua 5:10-15.

3. The children of Israel camped in Gilgal. What did they do on the fourteenth day of the month?

CONTINUED...

The observance of Passover was a time to celebrate and remember the LORD's faithful deliverance of the children of Israel from the bonds of slavery in Egypt. Forty years earlier, this celebration was given to the people to remind them that they were a redeemed people, set free by the mighty hand of their God. Describe the events of the Passover celebration as recorded in Exodus 12:1-28.

The people were to remember this day how they had been delivered from the slavery of Egypt. It was not by the strength of their flesh or their own ability but by the mighty hand of the LORD. Now, they faced a formidable enemy in Jericho. What was the Passover meant to teach Israel about the LORD and His relationship to them?

4.   The children of Israel ate the fruit of the land of Canaan on the day of Passover. The manna had ceased. God had kept His promise. He had brought them into the Land. This was just the beginning. For Israel, the Passover sacrifice pointed backward toward their redemption from Egypt. What do we learn about the New Covenant instituted by our Lord Jesus Christ as He celebrated Passover before His death?

a. Luke 22:14-20

b. 1Corinthians 5:7, 8

The following Scriptures remind us that we are not delivered from sin and death by anything we can do, but ONLY by the completed sacrifice at Calvary. It is also by Jesus' power that we are able to overcome temptation and the flesh, and walk in the Spirit. What encouragement do you find in these verses? How do they change your outlook today?

a. Ephesians 1:7, 8

b. Colossians 1:13, 14

c. 1Peter 1:18, 19

d. 1Peter 2:21-25

5. Joshua heads out to take a closer look at the walls of Jericho. Who does he encounter and what does he learn about this Man?

This Man whom Joshua met was Jesus Christ. The manifestation of God in the Old Testament is called a theophany. Joshua was about to lead God's people into to battle against many very strong opponents. Who was the Commander of the LORD's army?

According to Psalm 18:2-3, Who is the One Who fights your battles?

Seeing Joshua's behavior before the Commander of the LORD's army, what heart attitude characterizes a great spiritual leader?

6. Jesus Christ paid the full and complete penalty for every one of our sins. He bought us and brought us out of bondage. How often do you celebrate His finished work by observing Communion? Are you careful not to allow it to become a ritual or habit without true worship? Are you facing a battle – Who is the Commander in your life? Do you realize that you are always in the Lord's presence and always on Holy ground?

7. Record Joshua 6:16 here and continue to work on committing it to memory!

DAY 4 – BEGIN IN PRAYER

1. Read Joshua 6.

2. Read Joshua 6:1-11.

3. The people of Jericho were locked behind their walls and yet they were

CONTINUED...

terrified because they had heard what the LORD had done for the children of Israel. What declaration does the LORD make to Joshua in verse 2?

The work was complete; the LORD had given them the land. The history of the children of Israel stands as a type to us, as Christians. The redemptive work of Jesus Christ is complete; we have been given access to the promises. They belong to us, as His children. What do you learn from the following Scriptures regarding this finished work?

a. John 19:30

b. Romans 8:37

c. Ephesians 2:4-6

d. 2Peter 1:2-4

4. The people had been given the Land of Promise. But it would only become theirs as they entered in, in faith and obedience. What was the unique plan that was laid out for Joshua and the people to follow?

What a scene it must have been to watch this week long process. It certainly took great faith for Joshua and the people to follow the LORD's battle plan. They were learning one of the most important lessons we can learn as children of the Lord. What does Hebrews 11:30 teach us about this conquest of Jericho?

What more do we learn about faith and its powerful outcome?

a. 1John 5:4, 5

   b. Romans 5:1, 2

   c. Galatians 5:5, 6

5. So faith in the promises of the LORD caused this people to move out in obedience. Do you think it made sense? Do you think they understood God's plan? How does Isaiah 55:8, 9 speak to their circumstances?

    How does minister to you when you apply it to the circumstances in your life?

6. God has given you the victory through Jesus Christ! Will you enter in? Do you trust Him with the enemies in your life? Will you be obedient to His Word as you face the battle?

7. Record Joshua 6:16 here and continue to work on committing it to memory!

DAY 5 – BEGIN IN PRAYER

1. Read Joshua 6.

2. Re-read Joshua 6:12-27.

3. Joshua rose early in the morning and in faith and obedience he and the people followed the LORD's directions to the letter. What were they to do and for how many days were they to do it?

    What was to be different about the seventh day?

CONTINUED...

Where was the Ark of LORD to be placed in the procession? What might be the significance of this location?

What do the following Scriptures teach you about the Lord's presence among His people?

a. Deuteronomy 23:14

b. Isaiah 12:6

c. Zephaniah 3:17

4. Over two million people were in the nation of Israel, and marching them around the city of Jericho would have been quite an undertaking. The seven priests went first bearing seven trumpets of rams' horns. The Ark of the LORD followed them and armed men (soldiers) went before and behind. For a week the people obeyed quietly and what seemed like inaction must have been hard for this people who were known for their impatience. What lessons might they have needed to learn in this waiting? What lessons do we learn in the waiting?

The sound of the trumpet was a call to arms for the Israelites, and a warning to the people of Jericho. On the seventh day, after circling the city seven times, the people were to shout. Why? (v.16)

We, too, can shout for joy because the Lord has given us the victory. We can, or at least we should, shout for joy and praise the Lord even before we see the walls of the enemy collapsing before us! How can you apply the truth of the following Scriptures to the battles you are facing today?

a. 2Chronicles 20:20-22

b. Psalm 47:1-5

c. Psalm 98:4-9

d. 2Corinthians 10:4, 5

5. The city of Jericho was doomed. The LORD is long-suffering and merciful and yet judgment will come to those who reject Him. Jericho was an accursed city, the first representative of Canaan's evil. This people practiced every kind of sin and evil, and even though they had heard and seen the mighty power of God they refused to repent of their sin. Who was spared and why?

The LORD, through Joshua, reminded the people to be careful of the temptation that comes after the victory. It is at this time that the enemy often comes on strong seeking to wipe out God's people. What instruction was given regarding Jericho, her inhabitants, and her stuff?

Does the judgment seem harsh or are we seeing the Just and Holy sentence of the LORD who judges righteously?

How does 2Peter 3:1-10 speak of the Lord's mercy, love and righteous judgment?

"GOD IS PERPETUALLY AT WAR WITH SIN.
THAT IS THE WHOLE EXPLANATION OF THE EXTERMINATION OF THE CANAANITES."
G. CAMPEELL MORGAN

6. We can trust the Lord and shout the shout of victory even before we see the results of God's work in our circumstances. Will you praise Him for His faithfulness to carry you through today and bring victory in your life? The

CONTINUED...

lesson we learn from the LORD's dealing with the sinful Canaanites and His warning to "abstain from the accursed thing" is that He will tolerate no compromise with sin in the lives of His people. Is there any sin that has found itself welcome in your life? Today is the day of repentance!

7.   Record Joshua 6:16 here and continue to work on committing it to memory!

DAY 6 – BEGIN IN PRAYER

1.   Read Joshua Chapters 5 and 6. (You can do it! – It's important!)

2.   Write a prayer asking the Lord to use the truths in these to chapters to change and motivate your walk of faith with Him.

3.   Record Joshua 6:16 without looking!

DAY 1 – BEGIN IN PRAYER

1.   Read Joshua 7.

      What are the main details recorded in chapter 7?

      What stern warning is to be heeded from chapter 7?

2.   Read Joshua 8.

      What are the main details recorded in chapter 8?

      What lesson can be applied to your life from chapter 8?

3.   Use Joshua 8:1 as your memory verse for this week. Write it out and begin memorizing it today.

DAY 2 – BEGIN IN PRAYER

1.   Read Joshua 7.

2.   Re-read Joshua 7:1-15.

3.   The accounts of God's long-suffering love and patience are far more prevalent in the Bible than those of God's judgments. However, there are accounts of flagrant disobedience when we see God deal very quickly with sin. What sin had Israel committed and what were the affects of that sin?

      What similar judgment came upon the early church in Acts 5:1-11? Why do you think God dealt so quickly with sin in these two instances?

CONTINUED...

ENTERING *into* *His* **Promises**

Challenge: Can you find another example of God's immediate judgment against flagrant sin?

The LORD had clearly spoken through Joshua to the people concerning the accused thing. Everything in Jericho was to be either destroyed or consecrated to the LORD. What does God's Word teach us about the absolute necessity of obedience and whole-hearted worship without hypocrisy?

a. 1Samuel 15:22

b. Psalm 51:16, 17

c. Isaiah 1:11-20 (Summarize these verses)

d. Matthew 5:23, 24

4. After a great and mighty victory at Jericho in which the LORD proved to the people that He was the LORD of Hosts Who would fight their battles, we are given a clear outline for spiritual defeat. From the following verses of chapter seven, what are five causes for defeat that we should be very careful to avoid?

1.) Verse 1

2.) Verses 2-3

3.) Verse 4

4.) Verse 5

5.) Verse 7

5. Israel had sinned. They had transgressed God's covenant. They had stolen. Notice the corporate responsibility for allowing sin in the camp. According to

verses 11-15, what is the remedy for sin when we find ourselves separated from God's blessing because of our disobedience?

We serve a Holy and Just God Who cannot tolerate sin. Yet, we often treat sin lightly and allow it to dwell in our lives (sometimes we even nurture it). What is to be our attitude toward sin and how do we rid ourselves of it?

a. Romans 13:12-14

b. Ephesians 6:10-13

c. 1John 1:7-9

d. 1John 2:1-6

6. How has the Lord spoken to your heart this week regarding sin in your camp? Is there an accursed thing that you are hiding? Will you bring it before the Lord in repentance today? Your Heavenly Father is looking for obedience, not empty words or religious rituals. Allow Him to search your heart today and draw you closer to Him by removing those things that keep you from whole-hearted worship!

7. Record Joshua 8:1 here and continue to work on committing it to memory!

DAY 3 – BEGIN IN PRAYER

1. Read Joshua 7.

2. Re-read Joshua 7:16-26.

3. Achan was about to learn a crucial lesson that we should mark well and learn from. He was about to understand that no one could hide from God. His every thought and action were observed and recorded and the consequences

CONTINUED...

of his sin was about to be meted out. How do the following Scriptures illustrate this truth and how does it affect your life today?

a. Jeremiah 17:10

b. Jeremiah 23:24

c. Ecclesiastes 12:14

d. Psalm 139:7-12

e. Proverbs 15:3

4. So Joshua rose up early in the morning and the LORD methodically singled out the offender. First he chose by the tribe, then by family, then by household, and finally man-by-man until Achan was exposed. What attitude did Joshua show toward this man who had caused Israel so much grief, destruction, and shame (v. 19)?

What was Achan's response?

Food for thought & discussion: Was his confession too late? Do you think he was forgiven? Does forgiveness negate the consequences of sin?

Do you notice the progression of sin that trapped Achan? He saw, he coveted, he took and then he died! How do the following Scriptures illustrate this evil progression?

a. Genesis 3:6

b. 2Samuel 11:2-4

c. James 1:14, 15

5. Achan was guilty of stealing from the first fruits of the Lord. The punishment was severe and drastic. Since the law in Israel prohibited innocent family members from being punished for the sins of their relatives (Deuteronomy 24:16), we have to assume that Achan had drawn his family into his conspiracy. Sometimes people say their sin only hurts themselves and not others. Here Achan's sin led to the deaths of 36 innocent soldiers and all of his family members. The death penalty for this grave sin was a sobering lesson for 3 million onlookers that they (and we) are not to take God's Word lightly. Drastic measures were required. How does Jesus speak to this matter in Matthew 18:6-9?

6. What lesson has the Lord spoken to your heart today? Are there any changes that need to be made in your life? Will you allow the Lord to have free reign? What will you do to protect yourself from the evil progression of sin in your life? Need help? Read and practice Philippians 4:6-9!

7. Record Joshua 8:1 here and continue to work on committing it to memory!

DAY 4 – BEGIN IN PRAYER

1. Read Joshua 8.

2   Re-read Joshua 8:1-29. (No cheating!)

3. Chapter 8 begins with a fresh new relationship between the LORD and His people. Now they were willing to proceed God's way. They had tried it on their own and the result was utter failure. In verse 1 the LORD speaks to Joshua with these encouraging words, "Do not be afraid, nor be dismayed..." Joshua and the people had sinned and now they had found forgiveness and restoration. How does this encourage you when you think about the times you have fallen? How do the following Scriptures speak of the Lord's willingness to

CONTINUED...

forgive when we come to Him in repentance?

a. Jeremiah 33:8, 9

b. Psalm 32:1-6

c. Proverbs 28:13

d. 1John 1:9

4. Israel had judged the sin that had defiled their camp and now God would lay out the battle plan. A plan that would surely result in victory! What was that plan?

How many of the men of Israel were to be involved?

Why might the LORD have wanted all the army to be involved in this battle?

According to 1Samuel 17:47, who is the Lord of the Battle? Who is the Lord over those battles you are facing in your life today?

5. The detailed account of the victory at Ai teaches us that it is the Lord Who fights our battles and causes us to have victory. But at Ai, unlike Jericho, the people had the responsibility of being co-laborers with the LORD. God gave them the battle plan, but they had to be obedient to carry it to completion. Victory was complete, the enemy was destroyed; all the inhabitants of Ai were killed. Keep in mind that this was not the killing of innocent people but the judgment of God on an evil society that had long resisted God's grace and

truth. How does the account of this victory compare with the battle Moses and Joshua fought against the Amalekites in Exodus 17:8-16?

Sin has to be completely and utterly dealt with and destroyed in our lives and in our churches! What directions are we given that will guide us in obediently dealing with sin?

a. Galatians 5:24-26

b. Ephesians 4:22-29

c. Colossians 3:5-10

6. Do you truly believe that God offers forgiveness after you fall when you come to Him in repentance? Have you seen Him restore and bring victory from your failures? Is there a battle in your life that He has laid out a victory plan for you to follow? Will you be faithful to obey? Will you mortify the flesh and cast off any sin that lingers and put on the new man that is renewed day by day?

7. Record Joshua 8:1 here and continue to work on committing it to memory!

DAY 5 – BEGIN IN PRAYER

1. Read Joshua 8.

2. Re-read Joshua 8:30-35.

3. The victory was complete at Ai! Joshua led the people north to Shechem, which lies in the valley between Mt. Ebal and Mt. Gerizim. Here they were in the very center of the Promised Land! It was time for a renewal of commitment and renewal of surrender. According to verses 30 and 31, what did Joshua do here and why?

CONTINUED...

What do we learn from Deuteronomy 27:1-8 regarding Moses' instructions to Joshua and the people?

The people offered burnt offerings and peace offerings to the LORD in Mount Ebal. Burnt offerings were given wholly to God through fire and were offered to the LORD as a token of the nation's total commitment to Him (Leviticus 1). Peace offerings were an expression of gratitude to God for His goodness (Leviticus 3 and 7:11-34).

What act of consecration does Paul call for in the believer's life in Romans 12:1-2?

4.   The altar was to be made of whole stones, without any carvings made by iron tools. Why do you think the LORD commanded that the altar be made so simply?

What insight does Exodus 20:24-26 give us on the subject of the building of the altar?

How might 1 Corinthians 1:29-31 add important direction to us anytime we approach the Lord in worship or prayer?

Joshua was to write the Law on the stones so that they could be read and seen by all the people. They would be without excuse if they chose to disobey the Law. What does the New Testament teach about the Word of God and His Spirit in the life of the Christian?

a. John 16:12-15

b. Romans 8:1-4

c. 2Corinthians 3:2, 3

5. Joshua read all that Moses had commanded before all the assembly of Israel, men, women and children. Shechem is a natural amphitheater. The people were divided on either side of the valley and they were all facing the Ark of the Covenant, which represented God's presence among them. However, even if they had tried, the people would never be able to keep the Law, in fact the Law was given to prove our sinfulness and our need for a Savior. What do we learn from Galatians 3:19-26 about the Law and grace?

6. What is the extent of your commitment to the Lord today? Are you all in, or are you distracted by, or entangled with, the world? Are you daily adding His Word to your heart and life? Will you seek to be sure that all you think, do, and say brings glory to your Heavenly Father alone?

7. Record Joshua 8:1 here and continue to work on committing it to memory!

DAY 6 – BEGIN IN PRAYER

1. Read Joshua Chapters 7 and 8. (Once more – It's important!)

2. Write a prayer asking the Lord to use the truths in these to chapters two change and motivate your walk of faith with Him.

3. Record Joshua 8:1 without looking

Notes

DAY 1 — BEGIN IN PRAYER

1.   Read Joshua 9.

     What are the main details recorded in chapter 9?

     What lesson did Joshua and his men learn in chapter 9? How will it help you when you need to make decisions?

2.   Read Joshua 10.

     What are the main details recorded in chapter 10?

     What lesson can be applied to your life from chapter 10?
     (Is the enemy still dwelling safely in your life?)

3.   Use Joshua 9:14 as your memory verse for this week. Write it out and begin memorizing it today.

DAY 2 — BEGIN IN PRAYER

1.   Read Joshua 9.

2.   Re-read Joshua 9:1-14.

3.   Before we continue any further in our study of the conquest of the Promised Land, let's do a bit of review. What were Joshua and his army to do to the people in Canaan and why had the LORD given them such stern orders?

     a.   Exodus 34:11-17

     b.   Deuteronomy 7:1-6

CONTINUED...

ENTERING *into His* **promises**

JOSHUA 9 – 10

c. Deuteronomy 20:16-18

4. With the fall of Jericho and Ai, several kings joined in an alliance to fight together against the children of Israel. The Hivites were a part on this meeting but they decided on another plan to try to escape certain destruction. What was their plan?

Joshua and the people had just experienced great blessing in the defeat at Ai and it is at these times that the Christian needs to be prepared for a counter-attack. The enemy of Israel approached in a different manner, he came to deceive. He came subtly. He came lying. He came to destroy. What do you learn from the following Scriptures that will help you when the enemy attacks you?

a. John 8:42-44

b. 2Corinthians 11:3

c. 1Peter 5:8, 9

5. Joshua and the princes of Israel wrongly believed the lies of their enemy even though they were suspicious of their words. How does verse 14 sum up the serious problem?

We need to learn this lesson very well! The LORD would have shown them, if they had prayed. But they didn't pray! Use the following promises as a reminder that we ought always to seek the Lord's counsel for the decisions we make in our lives – big or small.

a. Proverbs 3:5, 6

b. Philippians 4:6, 7

c. James 1:5

6.   As believers, we daily face decisions that must be passed through the will of our Heavenly Father. What is obvious is not always correct! Are there areas in your life where you have compromised the truth of God's Word and made a covenant with people, possessions or activities that draw you away from the Lord? What will you do about them? Seek the Lord and obey His clear Word and He will give you His power to defeat the enemy!

7.   Record Joshua 9:14 here and continue to work on committing it to memory!

DAY 3 – BEGIN IN PRAYER

1.   Read Joshua 9.

2.   Re-read Joshua 9:15-27.

3.   Verse 15 says, "So Joshua made peace with them, and he made a covenant to let them live." He made peace with the enemy and it wouldn't be long before he was fully aware of his serious error. Use a Bible dictionary to define the word covenant in verse 15.

This same word is used to describe the relationship between the LORD and His people in Genesis 17:1-7. What do you learn about this covenant and how long would it last?

As Christians today, we live in a world surrounded by enemies of the Lord and enemies of the truth of His Word. We are clearly instructed to beware of any close attachment, ties, or covenants with the enemy. What do you learn from the following Scriptures about our relationship to the world and our alliances with the unbeliever?

a.   1 Corinthians 15:33

CONTINUED...

b. 2Corinthians 6:14-18

c. Ephesians 5:5-11

d. James 4:4

4. It wasn't long before Joshua and the princes of Israel discovered the sin they had committed. The children of Israel had traveled only three days when they came upon the cities with which they had made an alliance. The people were angry at the leader's decision, but it was too late. In Who's name was this covenant made?

Why do you think that they didn't just break the covenant?

Joshua and the leaders of Israel had to live with their covenant agreement. Even though they had been deceived, they did not want to bring further disgrace to the Name of the Lord. We, too, are to be faithful men and women of our word because our lives are to be living testimonies of our Lord Jesus Christ. Use the following Scriptures to lead and guide the words you speak and promises you make.

a. Ephesians 4:25-29

b. Colossians 3:8, 9

c. James 5:12

d. Psalm 19:14

Challenge: What happened in 2Samuel 21:1, 2 that tells us that Joshua and his men made the correct decision to honor their covenant with the Gibeonites? Do you think this applies to a Christian who promises to do things that God does not approve of? Why or why not?

5. The Gibeonites had heard that God had commanded Moses to destroy all the inhabitants of the land and they were afraid for their lives. They had decided that slavery was better than death. What role were they given to serve the children of Israel?

The city of Gibeon was given to the priestly family of Aaron, so it became a center for training in God's Word and worship. The Tabernacle would be placed in Gibeon for a time (2Chronicles 1:3, 5). A Gibeonite was among David's mighty men of valor (1Chronicles 12:1, 4). When the Jews returned from Babylon, the list of those who could prove their Jewish heritage included Gibeonites (Nehemiah 7:25) and we are told in Nehemiah 3:7 that they were among those who helped to rebuild the walls of Jerusalem. What do we learn about the nature and character of the Lord from the way things worked out for Gibeon?

Though we see the LORD bringing some good from the sin of presumption and lack of prayer on Joshua's part, should we ever assume we could disobey the Lord's clear Word and hope for the best?

6. Is there any area in your life that you are "unequally yoked?" What does the Lord require of you as a believer? Have you been true to your word? We are not to use God's grace as a cloak for sin! Will you ask the Lord to lead and guide you to be more obedient to His Word?

7. Record Joshua 9:14 here and continue to work on committing it to memory!

DAY 4 – BEGIN IN PRAYER

1. Read Joshua 10.

CONTINUED...

2.   Re-read Joshua 10:1-14.

3.   In chapter 10 we read of a summit of five kings of the Amorites. These kings were probably depending upon Gibeon, which was a great city, to help protect them from the advances of the army of the Israelites. Who led this alliance and what was to be their plan of attack (vs. 3-5)?

How did the Gibeonites respond to this threat of attack?

What lesson can we learn about making agreements, covenants or alliances with the enemy?

What exhortation did Paul write to Timothy in 2Timothy 2:4 that speaks to our need to be separate from the world?

4.   Already the treaty was making its demands. The Gibeonites ran to Joshua for help. When we make alliances with the enemy, we can expect to have to defend them in order to protect ourselves. Joshua quickly mobilized his fighting men of war and mighty men of valor. What words of encouragement and strength does Joshua receive on the journey toward Gibeon (v.8)?

How does Psalm 2:1-4 give us our Heavenly Father's perspective on those who choose to fight against Him and His people?

Joshua led his troops on an all night march trusting in a freshly renewed promise that the LORD was the One who would fight and win the battles. What promises have you and I, as believers, been given that should cause us not to fear when we face the battles in our lives?

a.   Matthew 28:20

b.   Romans 8:28-31

c. 2Corinthians 12:9, 10

d. Ephesians 1:19, 20

e. Philippians 4:6, 7

For Extra Blessings: Psalm 55:22. Psalm 103:11-13; Isaiah 43:25; John 10:27, 28; Philippians 4:19; Colossians 1:12-14 and 21,22; and 2Peter 1:3, 4.

5. The armies of Israel came face-to-face with the enemy after traveling all night. We are told that the LORD routed them before Israel. As they were on the retreat, what weapon did the LORD use against the enemy of Israel (v.11)?

Joshua sought a tremendous miracle from the LORD. It is recorded that this was a day like no other day! What happened?

Does it seem impossible? How do the following Scriptures explain this miracle?

a. Genesis 1:1

b. Psalm 33:6-9

c. Psalm 102:25, 26

d. Isaiah 45:12

Many seek to explain how it could happen but God's Word clearly declares

CONTINUED...

that nothing is too hard for the LORD who created and sustains it all!

6. Will you evaluate the alliances you have made and the ones you are considering making? Will you seek the Lord for His will in your choices? Even when we fail, the Lord is waiting to restore and bring beauty from ashes! How big is your God? What battles do you face today? Will you, like Joshua, trust God for a miracle?

7. Record Joshua 9:14 here and continue to work on committing it to memory!

DAY 5 – BEGIN IN PRAYER

1. Read Joshua 10.

2. Re-read Joshua 10:15-43.

3. The five enemy kings who had conspired and led this attack against Gibeon and Israel were captured. What instruction did Joshua give concerning these five kings (v.18)?

At the end of a miraculous battle, in which the LORD routed the enemy by using hailstones as weapons and stopped the sun and moon in the sky to allow for a complete victory, Joshua performed a public ceremony that gave encouragement and strength to his fighting men. An ancient custom called for victorious kings to put their foot upon the necks of the conquered. What reminder did Joshua give to his men regarding Who truly brought victory (v.25)?

According to 1Corinthians 1:27-31, when we find ourselves in a place of victory, Who is to receive the glory?

What do the following Scriptures teach us that we can glory in?

a. Jeremiah 9:23, 24

b. Galatians 6:14

4. The concept of the victor ruling and reigning over the defeated enemy is illustrated throughout Scripture. Since Joshua is a type of Jesus Christ, the spiritual application to the church is given to us through the following Scriptures. What do you learn?

    a. Psalm 110:1

    b. 1 Corinthians 15:24-28

    c. Ephesians 1:19-23

    d. Hebrews 2:7-9

5. Joshua clearly and publicly dealt with the five kings who led the attack against the children of Israel. But, this was not enough. His instructions from the LORD were very clear; he was to completely and utterly destroy the enemy. What enemy are we to completely and utterly destroy in our lives?

    a. Romans 8:13

    b. Galatians 5:24

    c. Colossians 3:5-9

    Food for thought: How is the Christian to deal with those who oppose us, and the Gospel of Jesus Christ today? See Romans 12:14-21.

6. Ask the Lord to reveal to you any areas in your life in which the enemy is still residing! Will you allow Him by His grace and mercy to utterly cast them out? You cannot fight these battles on your own – it is the Lord Who can and wants to bring total victory in your life!

CONTINUED...

7.   Record Joshua 9:14 here and continue to work on committing it to memory!

DAY 6 – BEGIN IN PRAYER

1.   Read Joshua 9 – 10.

2.   What warning is there to apply to your life today? What command is given regarding the enemy?

What promise is there of sure and certain victory to those who place their trust in the Lord Jesus Christ?

3.   Record Joshua 9:14 without looking!

DAY 1 – BEGIN IN PRAYER

This week's lesson differs from the others in that we will be covering much territory (literally & figuratively). These next nine chapters record the details of the conquest and division of the land among the tribes of Israel. We will read of victory in battle and numerous details about borders and geographical locations. Many of these cities no longer exist so we only know the approximate location. You may find them on a map with a question mark next to them. Therefore, this week we will be skipping through the chapters quickly and stopping to focus on the overall lesson of these chapters. To help you see the final division of the land find a Bible Map that shows the land of the twelve tribes of Israel.

1. Read Joshua 11.

2. In what area of the country had the previous battles (recorded in chapters 7-10) taken place?

3. According to verse 1, who steps up to lead the new wave of attacks against Joshua and the children of Israel?

   Where was Hazor located?

   How large was the enemy army?

   What did the LORD say to Joshua regarding the battle (v. 6)?

   How does Lamentations 3:21-26 encourage you as you face the enemy and the battles in your life?

4. What similar phrase or idea is repeated in verses 8, 11, 12, and 14?

   How must we, as Christians, apply this same practice to the enemies of our soul?

   What are these enemies according to Colossians 3:5-10?

CONTINUED...

into **ENTERING**
His **promises**

Personal: Which ones are still dwelling in your life? Ask the Lord Jesus Christ to begin to overcome these giants in your life!

5. Use Joshua 11:15 as your memory verse for this week. Write it out and begin memorizing it today.

DAY 2 – BEGIN IN PRAYER

1. Read Joshua 12-13.

2. In chapters 12-19 we are given greater detail of what happened during the battles and the division of the land. The chronological narrative is interrupted so that we get the details of the dividing of the land to each tribe, its borders, and the cities within its jurisdiction. These could be considered review chapters. In Joshua 11:18 we read that Joshua made war a long time with all those kings. According to 12:24, how many kings were defeated?

3. It had been about seven years since the first battle at Jericho. What do we learn about Joshua from 13:1?

    Read Joshua 11:23 along with Joshua 13:1. How can both of these statements be precise?

    Even though the land was inhabited and divided, much of the land was not fully liberated from the enemy. The LORD had made good on His promise to give Israel the land, but there was more work to be done on their part. How does this truth (that something can be ours even when we have not yet possessed it) apply to the Kingdom, which the Lord has promised to us, as His children?

4. There were still pockets and areas where the enemy continued dwelling in the land. The LORD again reminded the people that He would drive out these enemies (13:8) but they would have to obediently participate. The land was to be divided by the casting of the lot. According to Proverbs 16:33, Who rules in the casting of the lot?

As a Christian, what is your lot, portion and inheritance?

  a. Psalm 16:5-11

  b. Psalm 73:23-26

  c. Psalm 119:57

  d. Ephesians 1:11-14

  e. 1 Peter 1:3-5

5. Record Joshua 11:15 here and continue to work on committing it to memory!

DAY 3 – BEGIN IN PRAYER

1. Read Joshua 14-15.

2. Two and a half tribes remained on the other side of the Jordon (east of the Jordon). What was the circumstance involved in this choice according to Numbers 32:1-42?

What were the names of these two and a half tribes?

How was Joseph's inheritance divided?

CONTINUED...

3. Chapter 14 and 15 focus on the inheritance of the tribe of Judah. Find the tribe of Judah on your Bible map. From this tribe we are reintroduced to a man named Caleb, what was his history (14:6-14)?

How was his spiritual walk described?

What was his request?

What do you learn about the twelve spies sent in to the Promised Land and the outcome of their mission from Deuteronomy 1:21-38?

What more do you learn about Caleb from the following Scriptures?

a. Numbers 13:30

b. Numbers 14:24

4. Caleb had seen the giants at forty years of age, but he had seen them in light of the powerful God that he served. Caleb's heart was set on the Promised Land. He knew that God had preserved him for a purpose and at 85 years old he was no less ready to fight the enemy than when he was 40. What promise do you have from the Lord Jesus Christ empowering you for His service?

a. Romans 8:31-39

b. Philippians 4:13

c. Ephesians 6:10

In Joshua 15:63 we are told that the Judah could not drive out the inhabitants in Jerusalem. Given the promise of the LORD to give them the whole land, do you think that they could not or that they did not do it?

Personal: Has your faith in the power and might of the Lord Jesus Christ increased or decreased over the years? As the years pass, we should be growing more faithful and less fearful, continuing to boldly drive out the enemy wherever he is found! Would others describe your walk by saying, "he/she wholly follows the Lord?"

5.   Record Joshua 11:15 here and continue to work on committing it to memory!

DAY 4 – BEGIN IN PRAYER

1.   Read Joshua 16-17.

2.   In these chapters we are given the borders of the allotted land given to the sons' of Joseph, Ephraim and Manasseh. Find their land on your Bible map.

What was their complaint to Joshua regarding their portion? (17:14)

What was Joshua's solution to their problem? (17:15-18)

Did they follow his instruction? (16:10; 17:12)

3.   Rather than drive out the enemy and make room for growth, Ephraim and Manasseh chose to make peace with the enemy. In the same manner, we are sometimes tempted to make peace with the weakness of our flesh. We do so by justifying our sin and comparing it to others who are "worse than us." What are the works of the flesh that we should NOT allow in any form or fashion in our lives?

   a.   1Corinthians 5:9-13

CONTINUED...

b. Ephesians 5:3-5

c. James 4:1-8

4.　Knowing how Joshua dealt with the complaints of Ephraim and Manasseh, what lesson can we learn and follow when we are faced with people who murmur against God's provision? (Remember, the land was divided by the casting of lots and the control of the lot was in the LORD's hand).

5.　Record Joshua 11:15 here and continue to work on committing it to memory!

DAY 5 – BEGIN IN PRAYER

1.　Read Joshua 18-19.

2.　Verse 1 begins, "Now the whole congregation of the children of Israel assemble together at Shiloh," the name Shiloh means place of rest. Shiloh was about twelve miles south of Shechem in Ephraim's territory. What focal point of worship was set up in Shiloh?

What do we learn about the Tabernacle from the following Scriptures?

a. Exodus 29:42-46

b. Exodus 40:34-38

3.　What are we told about the progress of the taking of the land?

How many tribes had not yet received their inheritance?

©2004—MORNINGSTAR CHRISTIAN CHAPEL, WHITTIER, CA

It appears that they were slow to respond to the challenge and for this reason they hadn't gone to possess their land. Unlike Caleb, they seemed to lack the faith and zeal to step out. What strong words does Joshua have for the hesitating Israelites (v.3)?

How are you encouraged toward being more diligent in your walk from the following Scriptures?

a. Proverbs 12:11; 27

b. Proverbs 13:4

c. Romans 12:10, 11

d. Hebrews 6:10-12

e. 2Peter 1:5-11

4. Use the following references to make a list of the seven remaining tribes and use your map to locate their land.

18:11-28

19: 1-9

19:10-16

19:17-23

19:24-31

19:32-39

19:40-48

CONTINUED...

What inheritance would the Levites receive and why? (18:7)

5. Record Joshua 11:15 here and continue to work on committing it to memory!

DAY 6 – BEGIN IN PRAYER

1. Read and record the following verses:

Joshua 3:10

Joshua 13:6

Joshua 13:13

Joshua 15:63

Joshua 16:10

Joshua 17:12,13

Joshua 18:3

2. What warning is there to apply to your life today? What command is given regarding the enemy?

What promise is there of sure and certain victory to those who place their trust in the Lord Jesus Christ?

Personal: What enemy is still dwelling in your life? Will you by the strength and power of the Holy Spirit and the Word of God drive out the enemy beginning today?

3.   Record Joshua 11:15 without looking!

Notes

_____

_____

_____

_____

_____

_____

_____

_____

_____

_____

_____

_____

_____

_____

_____

_____

_____

_____

_____

_____

_____

_____

_____

_____

DAY 1 – BEGIN IN PRAYER

1. Read Joshua 20.

    What distinction is made between murder and manslaughter?

    What was established to protect the person who accidentally killed someone?

2. Read Joshua 21.

    What promise was fulfilled to the Levites and their families?

3. Read Joshua 22.

    What exhortation did Joshua give to Reuben, Gad and half the tribe of Manasseh (vs. 5, 6)?

    What did these tribes, who dwelt east of the Jordon, do that almost started a war?

4. Use Joshua 21:45 as your memory verse for this week. Write it out and begin memorizing it today.

DAY 2 – BEGIN IN PRAYER

1. Read Joshua 20.

2. What was the purpose of the "cities of refuge"?

CONTINUED...

ENTERING
into
His **promises**

How many of these cities were appointed in the Promised Land?

What were the names of these cities?

What more can you learn about the LORD'S instructions regarding the murderer, the manslayer, and the cities of refuge from Numbers 35:15-34?

3. The cities of refuge were necessary because society had no police force to investigate crime and therefore, it fell to the family to see to it that murders were avenged. What added detail are we given in Deuteronomy 19:1-6 that vividly teaches us about the mercy of the LORD in His care for His people?

How did this justice system demand rather severe judgment even to those who killed someone without hatred?

It is clear from this study that the killing of an innocent person is considered to be a terrible offense that polluted that land. The penalty for such a crime was death. The reason for the severity was that man is made in God's image and therefore his life is precious and should be treated with the utmost care. Read Genesis 1:26, 27. How do you think the loss of emphasis on this truth has adversely affected our society?

4. What connection is there between these cities of refuge and the One Who is the refuge of every sinner seeking protection from the enemy of soul?

How do these following Scriptures encourage you and give you rest?

a. Psalm 28:8

b. Psalm 46:1

PPc. Psalm 91:2-4

d. Hebrews 6:17-20

5.   Record Joshua 21:45 here and continue to work on committing it to memory!

DAY 3 – BEGIN IN PRAYER

1.   Read Joshua 21.

2.   According to the Word of God, the Levites were not to receive any land area, but were to be given cites and suburbs among the people to dwell in. In chapter 21 we are given the details of the assignment of forty-eight cities that were to be home to the priests and their families. According to the following Scriptures, what was the responsibility of the Levites toward the LORD and His people?

a. Numbers 3:6-8

b. Numbers 18:21-24

c. Deuteronomy 18:1, 2

d. Deuteronomy 31:9-13

3.   With the priest located among the people, their spiritual leadership would be found in every community. How has the Lord met this need for the Body of Christ today?

CONTINUED...

What is to be the ministry of those whom the Lord has placed in authority in the church today?

a. Acts 20:28-32

b. 1 Peter 5:1-4

4.   God had made a promise to Abraham 470 years earlier. Here we have a brilliant testimony to the faithfulness of God. God indeed honors His Word. It is certain, sure and it never fails. Use the following truths to strengthen your faith and encourage your heart as you patiently wait to see the Lord's promises accomplished in your life.

a. 1 Corinthians 10:12, 13

b. 1 Thessalonians 5:23, 24

c. 2 Thessalonians 3:1-3

5.   Record Joshua 21:45 here and continue to work on committing it to memory!

DAY 4 – BEGIN IN PRAYER

1.   Read Joshua 22:1-8.

2.   Joshua called before him the 2 1/2 tribes who had found the east side of the Jordon River to be a perfect spot for their families and their profession of raising cattle. They had been granted this land for a possession as long as they were willing to support their brethren in conquering the Promised Land. It had been over seven years since they had left their families. They had been faithful to their promise. Now they were free to return home. They were faithful to keep their word to Moses and Joshua because of their deep devotion to the LORD. How does their faithfulness stand as an example to you in your relationships today?

What instructions are we given regarding our responsibility to care for one another?

a. Philippians 1:27

b. Philippians 2:3-5

c. Galatians 6:1, 2

d. Colossians 3:14-17

3. Joshua's charge to the people in verse 5 is indeed the secret to a victorious Christian life. What was his exhortation?

How is this vital truth echoed throughout the New Testament Scriptures?

a. Luke 21:34

b. Hebrews 6:11, 12

c. 1 Timothy 4:16

d. 2 Peter 1:5-10

Personal: How would you rate yourself when it comes to the diligence with which you pursue intimacy and obedience in your walk with the Lord? What areas need to be surrendered? What attitude or activity needs to be forsaken? Will you lay aside those sins that so easily beset you and run to win?

CONTINUED...

4. Joshua blessed the troops and sent them back to their families with great spoils from the battles. According to verse 8, what responsibility did these men have toward their brethren who had stayed back to care for the families?

    According to 1Samuel 30:22-25, what similar ordinance was established during David's reign?

    What does 1Timothy 6:17-19 teach us about our material blessings and our responsibility to those who are in need?

5. Record Joshua 21:45 here and continue to work on committing it to memory!

DAY 5 — BEGIN IN PRAYER

1. Read Joshua 22:9-34.

2. Upon returning home, what decision was made by the 2 1/2 tribes east of the Jordon? What was the near outcome of this decision?

    What action was taken by the children of Israel upon hearing about the building of this altar?

    According to verses 15-19, for what purpose did the western tribes assume the altar was built?

3. Israel was concerned that if these 2 1/2 tribes rebelled against the LORD, the punishment for their sin would fall on the entire nation of Israel. Even though the Jordon separated them, they were still one people, one nation, with one God. What was the sin of Peor (Numbers 25:1-9)?

    According to Joshua 7:11, what was the sin of Achan?

4. Was rebellion, disobedience and idolatry the reason for the building of this altar?

What did the leaders of the eastern tribes say was the reason they decided to build the altar? (vs. 21-29)

5. How do you see the fear of the Lord represented in the lives of the children of Israel at this time in their journey?

What was the final outcome of this situation and how does it help to give us an example to follow when there is division among the Body of Christ?

What clear direction are we given to help deal with misunderstanding, conflict and division in the church?

a. Matthew 5:23, 24

b. Ephesians 4:24-29

How does 1Corinthians 12:12-26 speak about the absolute necessity of unity in the church family?

5. Record Joshua 21:45 here and continue to work on committing it to memory!

DAY 6 – BEGIN IN PRAYER

1. Re-read Joshua 21:43-45.

2. What has the Lord promised you as His child? Will you place your trust in His sure and certain Word?

CONTINUED...

3. Re-read Joshua 22:5, 6.

4. How will these verses guide you in your choices and decisions you need to make today?

5. Record Joshua 21:45 without looking!

DAY 1 – BEGIN IN PRAYER

1.   Read Joshua 23:1-10.

      What strong exhortation did Joshua declare to all of Israel's leaders?

2.   Read Joshua 23:11-16.

      What warning was given to the children of Israel regarding the temptation to turn back? What would be the consequences of such sin?

3.   Read Joshua 24:1-14.

      Who is the One Who accomplished the mighty works recorded in these verses? Who is it that promises to do the same in your life today?

4.   Read Joshua 24:15-33.

      What solemn choice did the people in the presence of Joshua make before his death? Is this the determination of your heart and life today?

5.   Use Joshua 24:15-16 as your memory verse for this week. Write it out and begin memorizing it today.

DAY 2 – BEGIN IN PRAYER

1.   Read Joshua 23: 1-10.

CONTINUED...

into
His
**ENTERING
Promises**

2. Joshua is nearly 110 years old. He had lived a long and victorious life and he had faithfully completed the work the LORD had called him to do. He was born in Egyptian captivity and now his life on earth was about to end. How and why would Paul's words in 2Timothy 4:7 be an apt description of Joshua's life?

Personal: If tomorrow you had to gather your family and friends about you and tell them the time had come for you to depart from this earth, what declaration could you make of your faithfulness? What needs to be done with more diligence? What needs to be attended to? Are there things you have neglected that will prevent you from declaring, "I have finished the work?"

3. Though Joshua was about to go the way of the earth, his greatest concern was not for himself. His greatest concern was for his people and their relationship with the LORD. Joshua, being a type of Jesus, foreshadows the work of the Messiah that was to come. Read John 17. What was Jesus' declaration of His ministry and His greatest concern just hours before He was to be crucified?

Joshua called for all the leaders to meet with him and he reminded them again of the faithfulness of the LORD. Though the enemies had been subdued, still they had not been fully rooted out. Joshua laid out before them two possible scenarios. What were they?

What warning is there to us regarding the enemies that seek to trap and destroy us today?

4. What strong exhortation did Joshua declare to his people in Joshua 23:6, 8?

The necessity of following Joshua's counsel is as important to us today as it was to the children of Israel. How does the New Testament clearly instruct us to hold fast to the LORD our God?

   a. 1 Corinthians 9:24-27

   b. Philippians 3:13, 14

   c. 1 Timothy 6:11, 12

   d. Hebrews 12:1-3

   Joshua 23:10 is a quote from Deuteronomy 32:30, which show us how well Joshua knew the Word of God. Who is it that fights your battles? Are you trying to go it alone? Read and meditate on Romans 8:31 and then walk in it by faith today!

5.   Record Joshua 24:15-16 here and continue to work on committing it to memory!

DAY 3 – BEGIN IN PRAYER

1.   Read Joshua 23:11-16.

2.   The Word of God is like a two-edged sword (Hebrews 4:12). God can bless and strengthen us by it if we choose to obey it, or He will chasten us until we surrender to it and submit to Him. The words of Joshua may seem harsh, but as long as we are in this body we will have to struggle against the flesh, which will seek to draw us back to the world. What warnings and exhortations do you find in the following Scriptures that will assist you in your choices today?

   a. Proverbs 4:23

   b. Luke 17:3, 4

CONTINUED...

   c. Luke 21:34-36

   d. 1Corinthians 10:12-14

   e. 1Timothy 4:16

3. Warning after warning is given to us through the Word regarding compromising with the world and its evil influences. How does 1John 2:15-17 completely describe the world and its stuff?

   According to James 1:13-16, what is the process of temptation and what is the end result of following this process?

4. Moses had warned the children of Israel against compromise with the enemy and now Joshua reaffirms that warning. The LORD would be faithful to keep His Word and fight their battles for them, but if they chose to turn their backs on the LORD and serve other gods the consequences for the transgression would be grave. It was Charles Spurgeon who said, "God will not allow His children to sin successfully." Record Galatians 6:7,8 as a reminder to take careful heed to yourself. Use it to evaluate how you are sowing and what you will be reaping. Are there changes that need to be made?

5. Record Joshua 24:15-16 here and continue to work on committing it to memory!

DAY 4 – BEGIN IN PRAYER

1. Read Joshua 24:1-13.

2. Joshua had first gathered the leaders and exhorted them to love the LORD with all their hearts and to obediently follow Him, keeping themselves

unstained from the enemy that dwelt among them. Now he gathers all the tribes of Israel at Shechem. Shechem was a very significant location in the history of this people. Shechem was where God had promised Abraham that his seed would inherit the land (Genesis 12:6, 7). It was here that Jacob purchased a plot of land, and here where the bones of Joseph would be buried We read in Joshua 8:30-35 that the people had reconfirmed their complete devotion to the LORD at Shechem. Now, it is the place of Joshua's farewell address to the people. He begins with a direct Word of prophecy from the Lord beginning in verse 2. Who is the main subject of these thirteen verses?

Why do you think it is important for the children of Israel, and you and I today, to be continually reminded of all that the Lord has done on our behalf?

The LORD had chosen Abraham out of Haran and promised him and his decendants an inheritance. Likewise, He has chosen the believer out of the world and rescued us from the bondage of sin and death. What do we learn about this choosing and how does it strengthen your walk today?

a. John 15:16

b. Romans 8:30

c. Ephesians 1:3, 4

d. 1 Peter 2:9

Personal: Do you too often take His sacrifice of love for granted? Rehearse your history today. How far has He brought you? Where might you have been? Will you give Him the praise, honor and devotion He deserves, daily?

CONTINUED...

3. The Lord led His people from bondage bringing them into the land of the Amorites and the Canaanites. He fought their battles and gave them victory. To the believer, His promises are still the same. If we allow Him to reign in our hearts, He will lead and guide our every step and fight our every enemy. What promises of victory are yours today?

    a. Proverbs 3:5-8

    b. Galatians 2:20

    c. Galatians 5:16

    d. Ephesians 6:10-13

4. In verse 13, the LORD told the people that He had given them the land...a land for which they did not labor, and cities that they did not build. They were reminded that all that they had, and would be given, came as generous gift from the hand of God. The same is true for the Christian today. What do we learn from James 1:17 about every good gift?

    Selah: A heart controlled by gratitude and thanksgiving is a strong defense against the temptations the come from the flesh, the enemy and the world.

5. Record Joshua 24:15-16 here and continue to work on committing it to memory!

DAY 5 — BEGIN IN PRAYER

1. Read Joshua 24:14-33.

2. Re-read Joshua 24:14-33 and note the number of times Joshua uses the word serve. In verses 14 and 15 Joshua calls for a choice to be made, each individual is given a call to choose who he will serve. Based on the history that Joshua had just reminded them of, the choice should have been obvious. What decision did this people have to make? (v. 15)

What was Joshua's decision for him and his family?

What was the people's response (vs. 16-18)?

3. Three times the people confirmed their devotion to the LORD. Who would be a witness against them if they turned back from their commitment (v. 22)?

What did Joshua do that would help to remind them of the covenant that they made before the LORD?

What about your walk with the Lord Jesus Christ today? Do you declare boldly with Joshua, "As for me and my house we will serve the Lord?" What was Peter's response to the Lord's question to the disciples in John 6:67-69?

According to the following Scriptures, what priority is to be given to our love and commitment to the Lord?

a. Matthew 10:37-39

b. Mark 12:29, 30

CONTINUED...

    c. Luke 9:23-26

    d. Philippians 3:7, 8

4.   Three burials are recorded in these final verses of the Book of Joshua. We read, "Now it came to pass after these things that Joshua the son of Nun, the servant of the LORD, died, being one hundred and ten years old. And they buried him within the borders of his inheritance at Timnath Serah." How long, thereafter, did Israel serve the LORD?

    Why didn't the next generation know the LORD and what He had done for Israel?

    How can we prevent history repeating itself in our generation?

    a. Deuteronomy 6:6-9
    (This was the command that the children of Israel ignored – let's not do the same!)

    b. Ephesians 6:4

5.   Record Joshua 21:45 here and continue to work on committing it to memory!

DAY 6 – BEGIN IN PRAYER

1.   This Bible Study is entitled, "Entering into His Promises," and often when teachers speak of the Book of Joshua the believer is exhorted to "posses his possessions." Let's read a few Scriptures today that speak of the promises and possessions of the believer in the Lord Jesus Christ. It is not enough to know you have been given these possessions; we must learn to appropriate them.

2.   Read and meditate on the following portions of Scripture. Don't write anything down yet!

    a. Ephesians 1:3-11

    b. Ephesians 2:1-10

    c. Colossians 1:12-14

    d. Colossians 2:9-15

3. Are there some of these promises you cannot truly believe to be true? Beginning today, daily ask the Lord to give you the faith to possess your possessions, because they are truthfully yours, God's Word tells you so, and He does not lie and He never changes!

4. These are just some of the possessions you have in Jesus Christ. Record 1 Peter 1:2-4.

Search His Word diligently and find out what you're missing!

5. Record Joshua 24:15-16 without looking!

www.ingramcontent.com/pod-product-compliance
Lightning Source LLC
LaVergne TN
LVHW081348060426
835508LV00017B/1475